Words
Like
Love

Tanaya Winder

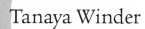

for hearts that collide

this was written for us
for those who believe in the healing of broken hearts
and for anyone who has ever shattered,
may this be a constellation to help guide you back to yourself.
for those who need a way back into love.

Published with the generous support of the City of Albuquerque's
Urban Enhancement Trust Fund

Words Like Love

First edition: August 2015
Paperback ISBN 978-0-9910742-7-3
West End Press / P.O. Box 27334 / Albuquerque, New Mexico 87125
For book information, see our website at www.westendpress.org

Book design by Lila Sanchez
Cover art by Angela Sterritt

Table of Contents

III. Forbidden Acts

IV. The Order Of Things

I. LESSONS IN FRAILTY

I have to tell you something, I said. I'm not going to lie. I have to tell you. I have this God-shaped hole in my heart, and I think you do too.

— Richard Van Camp, *The Lesser Blessed*

i write this without breaking my heart
#mantra

dear moon

hallow out my memory to a tree trunk
turned canoe so I may sail away from
the sea of you, waiting, ready to burst
into Milky Way. indistinguishable pieces
every time my mouth opens to encircle
your name but my lips dare not

form the shape.

reflections of the moon

in the beginning, Earth yearned for a companion, the Sun,
someone to share in the gifts: land, water, and
life. even light needs balance, darkness, death

to understand the push pull, days
echoing continuously. so, Earth gave an offering
to the sky, to become the Moon.

ever since, the sun dreams growth
believing we would know – love intertwined
with loss if only we would look up each night.

but, we buried Earth's sacrifice, caught in
our own wayward wanderings.
the stars aren't the only ones capable of falling

the weight of water

I.

When I first arrived into this world, I flew
on ancient winds. I was born into a creation story.

II.

Long ago, my great great great grandmother met
her other half. He, too, flew on winds, then as one of
many grains of sand – each split in half looking
        for the other. Back then, humans were only spirits

searching for connections. Long ago, a single grain found
another, my grandmother. So, they asked the Creator
for bodies, to know what it was like to touch each other.
They did and foresaw their child would die in birth.
        So they prayed – Save her, each sacrificing

something in return. The man entered the spirit world
as a horse and the woman opened herself up
from the center to give him a piece of her
        to remain connected.

III.

In the middle of the desert
there is a lake created out of tears. Long ago
there was a mother with four daughters:
North, East, South, and West. Once they grew up
each daughter left to follow her own direction.

Saddened by this loss, the mother cried
so intensely the skies envied her ability to create
such moisture. Days turned to months, months to
years and tears gathered in salty pools that gravitated
towards each other's weight. Unable to release
her bitterness, the mother turned to stone.

Today, the Stone Mother waits.
Come back to me my children.
Come back to me.

in my mother's womb

i.

i came into this world
incomplete, born with a hole
in my heart. it happened

in my mother's womb.
doctors have a name for it:
call it *congenital cardiovascular defect.*

my grandmother says *it's the moon
emptied of its many faces.* it is against nature.
creation has a will of its own.

or is it a pact from the past
made long ago? it happened
in my mother's womb, the blood

vessels closest to my heart
didn't develop the way nature
or the Creator intended.

when the doctors say *hereditary*,
my grandmother responds
ancestrally — in prayer, songs gifted

to her like birds. my mother and i do not know
the words. but, when grandmother sings
she is calling on horses to run in on clouds

to protect us, to save us.

ii.

long ago, there was a man
who loved my great great great grandmother.
the love connected two people, two

spirits so deeply it shook the earth.
i imagine it, the way it should have lasted
long after the moon. yet, he left her.

his leaving made
this hole passed down
in my grandmother's grandmother's womb.

lessons in frailty

At grandmother's house we played with paper
dolls, punched along perforated lines. Dressed in
their best, tabs held secure, our dolls formed choirs
to sing about the space between raindrops, the
pockets of stillness. In the storm's thickness there
are pauses to recover from inevitable wear.

Then years slip away,

dolls tatter, but grandmother refused defeat. We
glued broken arms, taped together small tears but
they seemed to rip further the more carefully we
held. Paper doll messengers intent on teaching
process: fold and release.

We wandered generations

in that two-dimensional realm where we didn't
know indentations would remain, that we'd search
for decades trying to figure out when grandmother
became silent as paper,

aging beyond repair

handling paper dolls

sometimes the world sees us as 2-
dimensional, as object, a Tiger Lily catering to

Peter Pans. one would never ever guess that
in this land young girls would need to be taught

how easy it is to be ripped, torn, and worse,
taken away. Never Never Land-

ing home after being stolen, swept under the rug
someone else's hands covering our mouths.

a story about winter

when I ask: why I was born in December?
Mother tells me about the Winter

Bird. When all others can't stand the cold
and bitterness, they leave, fly away

to places without pressures, the desolation
this world buries. But the Winter Bird stays

through the coldest winters. She does
not give in. This is how mother helps me

understand no one lives life unscathed.
In preparation, she bathed me, slowly turning

her baby again and again in snow,
in cold. Grandmother foresaw my voice

scattered snowflakes destined to inhabit sky.
With snow's shawl wrapped around me like centuries,

I could withstand the weariness of my winters.
After she gifts me her story, I become obsessed

with heaviness like a road to forgiveness or
reconciliation. Then I did not know December

would be when we lost grandfather or trauma
would coil around us all, so tightly we'd

freeze. I did not know grief would bring me
to knees praying: I cannot be afraid of the winters

inside me. The story rises like smoke welcoming
the thirst: grow wings and begin the journey home.

one day you will encounter a house flooded

there are no drains or lifeboats
      to save you, rather dozens of ships
          inside bottles, mast less. within the glass
               boundaries

            you built them in your image:
        impractical, on the brink of
capsizing. each time you let yourself fall

            the stability in his voice
          threaded through the holes
      within you. one slight tug

of the string heaved you into
      unhinged, then it was onto the next,
          a new thread, a new threat. you bottled up
               moments

            thinking love could be
        salvaged, tried to fill
windless sails with whispered

            wishes: *castaway, castaway,*
        just enough to propel you
to the next shatter. it wasn't such

a bad track record: you only fell
      in love about 35% of the time not wanting
          to be pulled like tides or lose control.
               anchored in

illusion you ruined your own
rigging to risk drowning
in make-believe; it was so much easier

to pretend to fall in love.
when you were young
you couldn't see your actions

coincided with leap years
though it was never about the jump
or fall. not at all. back then, you didn't know
you were born

with rivers already flowing
inside you. when you find yourself
in a house with water rising:

do not fear dying.
spread your arms
to lengths wider

than sorrow could ever reach.
embrace the collapse. free the parts
that feed the heart in you that will always be
a thirsty, overflowing ocean.

the stone mother

i.

I spent my childhood floating
on my back, steady in between,
        the sky, sun, moon

all of creation above me
and the lake, beneath. There is a peace
        in being carried by waves.

ii.

How much we do not let go of
when we carry the weight of water,
        the tears around us, in a generation

out of balance. We carry Stone
Mother's cries, *come back to me,* in our hair
        thick enough to clog drains
                and water rises.

surrender to memory

pieces cannot be separated so easily
                    mother once told me with hands
parting hair. *Twist. Turn. Wrap. Hook.*

How long it takes each piece to become
capable of braided conversation. We cut shorter, closer
                    to the source. With loss, we twist.

Mother cut by inches when her mother died.
                    Some things can be measured: miles,
minutes, growth in inches, each year we travel.

Memories unravel like turns in rivers
our ancestors helped us navigate with stars during seasons,
                    but in loss our mothers taught

                    crisscross nights with days. In a braid
                              tightly plaited we know futures flow
in strands. Wrapped with present and

past, our lives hook and unhook like hands
trying to hold on and simultaneously surrender to
                    what's measured in strands.

softly: how to evaporate

water into memory?
        It begins with curtains
                annoyed by their own lace

white against white,
        the snow outside,
                and you. In the kitchen

washing dishes, we
        don't talk about morning
                or day, the weeks to come

the cruelty, the plainness
        of waking and sleep.
                Accustomed to routine

                        we forget meals eaten, dishes
        broken over time. A temporary
bowl of hands submerges

                        carefully like this
        water slips through
the crevices, the same

                        fleeting hummingbird in winter,
        slow and awkward unable
to bear its own weight.

after, life

I've become obsessed with death rituals where relatives
jump into rivers. Some say it must be the nearest body of

water, even in winter, ice fractured, surface splintered.
When someone dies others say do not bathe for days, a week;

the cord from before still clings to worn sweaters, unwashed
jeans, to things once considered familiar, the body's

predictable waking. Routine: wash face, brush teeth, the
swift unnoticed gestures, hand sweeps hair behind ear, away

mirrors should be covered too. The unplanned cracks as
earthquakes wait patiently. You rarely see eruption coming,

but *after* after eats at the living like a river carves mountain,
leaving the living exposed, a sound unable to swallow itself.

the textures of silence

      in snowflakes' descent
from Heaven to Earth, the solitude stretches across distances
a symphony walking on snow, footsteps frozen
Earth's knowing covers the land in
      the eventual melting to come.

II. LANGUAGE LESS LEARNING

Her belief in the power of love to transform everything is so strong;
it blinds her to reality.

— bell hooks, *Wounds of Passion*

i write this without breaking
#myheart

broken/pipelines
#environmentalviolence

if we

cannot even love	our land
how can we love	each other
how can we love	our/selves

raw

Once we broke down at a gas station. Mom put coolant into the car as a woman approached. In her arms a blue cooler much bigger than her small frame. I thought she was going to fall over from the weight of it, arms coiled tightly around her precious cargo. As she got closer she revealed small packages wrapped in white paper and masking tape. An exchange of words, a hug, and then a hand off—cash for ten packages.

What did she want mom? What's in those packages?
Meat.
Meat?
Frozen, raw meat.

Turns out, the woman was getting beaten by her husband. Punched, kicked, fist to her cheeks until her skin rubbed raw. This went on for years until this morning. She decided it was the last morning. He'd given her a shiner on one side, a black eye on the other.

Routine: Open the freezer. Grab a steak. Place on face. Help reduce visibility of the bruising. But, today with flesh on cheek she decided to wrap every single piece of meat in her freezer, put it in a cooler and take whatever she made to get away.

Why'd you buy meat from a stranger?
So that she could finally leave.

Sonnet MCLXXXI

for the murdered & missing Indigenous women on Turtle Island

Not when or where but *how,* did we lose you,
in between *Last Seen* _____the words become elegy
echoing sidewalks and streets. Hand out your picture to
strangers. Post it on Post Office bulletin boards: *Missing*
as if it were destination, a place one goes
to disappear in invisible cities. Except there's no hero like
in the movies. No ads, mainstream coverage, or TV shows
to show our story. Are we invisible if no one knows, why?
When 1,181 women were taken, did eyes cease to have vision
or pay attention to a body being swallowed up?
Those left behind who remember you continue on a mission,
an endless search of the cities in which we loved
(and love) you. We will never forget. We demand for you
action, words, even a poem that ends: your lives matter, too.

sculpt-her

I finally understand object--i--fying.

i am flying away from myself.

i object to death

as if it were a ruling a decision made for me long ago

object--i--fi--ca--tion moving in motion

an action derived from colonization an aftermath

syrup-thick oil destroying the body of our mother

displaced into man camps or costume Pocahottie

not me

"this is *not* me" on repeat to daughters witnessing trick or

treat on the streets human trafficked

sex worker choices made or made for you

cope by turning tears into glass, a veil separating

the event, the person. make her sculpt--her, indestructible

as stone. a lost soul, fortify her, us, them all of this,

in paper,

frail, flimsy, I flail in waters of weighted grief. fear i am more

afraid to drown in releasing.

object--stone. mother--marble.

if you crafted your death does that make it

artful? i unlock my jaw mouth enough space to empty

a wail at depths i did not know tones could reach,

begging for the horses to run in on winds.

save me save us before i become stone, numb,

before i freeze screams into a seashell

i must hold to ear to hear the sounds of

water finally breaking.

the impermanence of human sculptures

the essential arrangements:
choose a coffin

to keep her
protected

from the elements. Consider the palpable
aging of paper, given sufficient time

we rust like iron, disintegrate
in the presence of air

moisture and water.
Do we all sleep like marble

statues, fixed points
in a room with locked expressions?

Interpreting the abstract
space dangling

between waking and
sleeping is an obsessive repetition.

Was it Eva Hesse
who explored the medium of art

fading over
time

and wasn't that part of
what made it

beautiful? That's what I still called my mother
post-mastectomy, her single breast

a perfect display of three-dimensional
impermanence. A brave faced statue,

that's how I like to think of it. No—
that thinking makes it bearable

when people ask: how
did it happen? She hanged herself, a lone

wire suspending her delicately
like wet paper molded into the exact shape

of emptiness, unstable
like paper

left crumpling in the wind,
or Eva. Dear Eva,

diagnosed with a brain tumor, Eva
who died in 1970

and mother who left
behind words: keep it, safe —

as if situations and places
as if names and people

couldn't rust into
indistinguishable blurs.

entering the age of doubt

what do we make   of a world   obsessed   with trying

to take and transform, until what is natural becomes

unnatural. who would believe   earth's tears

would gather in   salty whirlpools   gravitating

towards   each other's   weight or that

an Age of Doubt   came   from wanting.   Too much

wishing upon stars   shaken   into silence. When

the unlikely occurs: earth splits herself   open

from the inside   birds fall from skies   a presage

to the Age of Silence   where intoxicated glaciers   stealth

slowly, radiating   across   the land   in

unforgiving rivers,   the troubled waters

that eventually   cover up   our names.

w(hole): self-medication

Sipping on sorrows in search of hidden arias at the bottle's bottom,
the partygoers like conductors and we're all in the chorus.
Every time a hand picks up bottle to lips it's a gesture so graceful
you'd think an orchestra was being led in legato, we are all tied
together in our slurred performance. Each note deep within us
feeding desire. Empty the glass, tip another bottle up. The hand
held in midair, a conductor signaling: take a final breath before
we begin. Drowning in barely recognizable moments,
what happens when no one's looking.
The things we don't like to read about
in headlines: domestic abuse violence or rape or the child left
behind. Jacked up on Jack someone falls asleep on a bench or car
only to be frozen to death. Maybe we were never supposed to feel
cold's cadence, never supposed to yearn to feel
something warm inside us. The way coffee heats one up
from the inside, the way love
when it's done right, will serenade warm energy
rather than the imagined rapture, the staccatoed prodding
of someone searching for holes within you. They sense brokenness
seeping out like water, dogs hungrily lapping up laments. Regret,
bitterness lingering long after on our tongues, mourning the holes
inside ourselves, unaware it's each other's emptiness we feel,
thinking we can fill it with continuous crescendos,
bottles clinking like wishes for reversal, to change
the score: if only we could try this again,
knowing how the music ends.

when we banish tongues

i.
we've entered a New World
Order on words, days
of economic deprivation
where only one percent thrives.
time is dictated by greediness
and fear, days when books
are banned by the belief
consumed. unnerved
from tainted verbs,
smallpox blankets waiting
to infect them with brownness,
as if it seeps through pages
it's become contagious
to their white space.

ii.
the world changed
from childhood where i roamed
aisles, books stacked high
reaching for titles, birds to carry me
into other worlds. lift me into flight.

iii.
destination: past.
remember though we've been tortured, raped,
and burned, we always come back.
even when they try to silence cries
the classroom caged bird still sounds a song.

iv.
didn't we first start losing ourselves
with tongues banished? if we bury all books
containing atrocity will that change
history? this has happened before.
if history repeats itself i worry about
the children i have
yet to have: will i
be able to read to them
in bed at night? will they wake up
asking: where are the books?

v.
where are the books?
what happened to them? What
will I read my children? and where?

vi.
classroom banished words
become contraband. so i will
put bird ready-messengers
to paper, hold my piece
in my mouth until words
migrate out.

though their wings may ache
with oppression, they'll recite oral histories
hidden in the constellations,
we will tell our children
we needed the entire sky
to tell our story
the blank page

just wasn't
enough
space

learning to say *i love you*

my favorite conversations are with my grandmother while she
teaches me words in "Indian" as she says. I ask,

how do you say, *where did you go?* and *where are you going?*
Questions that layer my tongue in ash, reminding me of fire,

the taste. Each time I speak, the slow burn of every loss I have
witnessed cracks my lips. Go and going – acts singed

into my bones so I ask. Teach me *I'm coming with you* so it sits
rock heavy in my mouth because my tongue is at war

with history, boarding school "Kill the Indian, Save the Man"
acts of colonization. Strain pronunciation. When I want to say,

take me with you   it **dis so**   l   v   e   s

before I can stomach the sweetness of language. Ours,
I am losing. I am lost lodged somewhere in my throat

between decades of **bro   ken   syl   la   bles**. Teach me
how to reach the ones who are born already running.

Teach me how to talk to the ones who need it most.
Dear Universe, gift me words

that   l   i   n   g   e   r

softly like dusk. There must be a phrase to contain
wherever you go whether or not you know where you've been

or where you are going. She says, This is how to say:
I love you, a north star to always navigate coming home.

language less learning

i.
the words leave my body like moths,
dismantling wings – X means X, Y means Y

and V speaks volumes when my daughter asks:
have our languages died? I know no other way to say

some are dead. Our dying manifests
its destiny on the blank page of a poem

that should be titled "Once Spoken By A Woman
Who No Longer Speaks Her Language"

She would see how daunting
the white space is

ii.
the words lost in the dirt-ridden floors of her former
boarding schools, where they taught *make it new, make it*

new. Words enforced by a man who wanted us to be modern.
Maybe it was too difficult to be real

or the reality too harsh in trying to find oneself.
How to be American in America questioning

what it means to dream and at the same time
defer to the appropriation

of language. I'm envious. My daughter, I wish I could write
a poem in my native language. But grandmother,

the last one who speaks it, doesn't know how
to write it, and here I sit not knowing

how to type in anything
other than English.

crazy eight: keeping pace

Action. Let the portrayal begin —
Ridiculous headdresses. *in whose honor*

is it when you've already set the scene: derogatory.
Sandler's "satire" when he's calling all the

shots. hollywood's holy indian. urban
outfitters outfitted with smudge kits

how easily they try to "bless" away the boundaries
of appropriation like a game

you forfeit the ball. each time you step
one foot outside the white line

surrounding the space you must remain in.
we've seen it. referees calling us

on moves we didn't make:
blood quantum, boarding schools, or

assimilation, staying inside the paint too long.
we thought of it as war,

colors to spread across our cheeks, a sign of bravery.
unafraid to stand our ground we've posted up

below the goal, listening to the point guard,
the chief in charge, dribble that ball

repetitiously *boom boom boom*
trying too hard to keep pace

with a heart   beat   like drum powwow
pounding prayers into the ground

what john wayne couldn't have known

There are consequences to showcasing painted faces
in this world where we remain nameless,

   Injun, Savage, Squaw the list goes on. Characters frozen,

framed against a generation where some believe
the only good Indian is still a dead one.

   As children we used to watch movies *"Blood In, Blood Out,"*

growing up we knew blood was all about how much:
½, ¼, the breakdown of a whole. Like a pie cut

   into slices, the pieces define us. Fragmented, we've

been searching for how to make ourselves complete. We
weren't raised dancing with wolves, pre-*Smoke Signals*

   films meant to capture our experience. No more

days watching Westerns with John like those who
came before were forced to cheer for the army. No,

   we found comfort in movies like *"Mi Familia,"* *"Mi Vida Loca"*

pretending we were them, wishing for one language, one
movement to unite our many tribes. Instead

   we became scribes. Pen in hand, sometimes a knife,

we'd write our identities into our skin, carve: 3 dots present,
future, past on our hands. And it's no joke Indians love country.

John couldn't have known that later we would sing along

with cowboys, we've gone country still waiting
for the rest of America to get back to her roots,

maybe a little crazy, too in trying to remember how

did we get here, to where we privilege icons over
remembering how we even got our names.

ten little indians

one in three Native American or Alaska Native women will be raped at some point in their lives

sometimes the story is told differently: *one little, two little, three little indians*
or not told at all. most know one story about indian boys torn
between reservation and cities. tradition:
bear   root   sage   drumbeats
history and what's left?
bear turned to beer

dances to drunken driving, the stereotypical drunken indian
and maybe we're all gambling our lives away *four little,*
five little, six little indians and it's not just the boys,
but our princesses too. per capita
has made some greedy. for blood
quantum has turned us needy,
craving to make ourselves whole.

babies born into broken wombs, in a community
where ten little indian boys should learn
how to be men. instead, we ask:
do they remember? how
to touch a woman

with respect. the old dances taught us,
she chooses you *seven little, eight little, nine little indians,*
ten little indian boys sit on the bus listening –
their older cousins joke and tease, "see…
that girl in baggy sweats about to get on?
she had a train pulled on her this weekend."

they laugh, the little indian boys do, not knowing someday
not too long from now men will gather around a fire
singing forty-nine songs about

love. maybe their father's never taught them
how to touch her, that loving her didn't mean taking her
blacked out where she wakes up not remembering, not remembering:

> *ten little, nine little, eight little indians,*
> *seven little, six little, five little indians,*
> *four little, three little, two little indians.*
> *one little indian boy.*

sometimes i dream a reservation resides inside me

A reservation resides inside me

        its borders, a river so lonely it floods

the boundaries separating us.

              No one in the dream asks how many

reasons we have left, there is nothing

        to be quantified. I dream

           there are words inside me so anxious

they jump because they're stuck

        in my heart dying to be given breath.

I swallowed them years ago

           on open fields as I tried to shout

on plains, watching the slaughtered

        hearing the screaming rapes of my children's

        children, my sisters. The aftermath of

silence was learned in boarding schools, the words

        I couldn't release,

three generations later, no longer know

        how to navigate a way to come out.

intertribal

So many heartsongs to give voice to
When I was a child   When I was a child   When we were children
our past in refrains, waves that break against the sands,
our history. In my mouth the taste of winter
and when I speak, I speak winter
When I go to sleep I whisper
remember. Remember,
remember,
re-member

III. FORBIDDEN ACTS

"Our love died where the beats collide."
—Frank Waln, "Runaway"

i write this without
#breakingmyheart

forbidden acts

Culture said it was forbidden
to see a lunar eclipse, but you did it anyway,
watched it on the solstice.

We imagined the sun
embarrasses the moon to weep and saw a sky
full of stars, in their stillness

wrapped as delicate, edible songs
waiting to be placed in palms. We believed we could
sing them loud enough to cross destinies

if we shook hands with sorrow
by blowing kisses to the stars every night. After, you dreamt
butterflies could gather

enough dust to turn into
birds that carry you away from my life, yours,
and into the next.

the war on words

Somewhere a man and a woman read poetry to each other
lying in bed. They know this isn't the first time

her and his-stories have been bound like two fists:
colonized by invisible handcuffs. Versed in subversive

tactics, oral traditions of reading in-between the lines,
the man and the woman occupy their bedroom.

Banned books stacked as nightstands; he reads to her
The Pedagogy of the Oppressed as she cups her own breast.

They learn about their bodies, their own incompleteness,
in re-thinking Columbus. They move from book to book.

Stories strung out in bloodlines leading back to borderlands.
Everyone is testing faith these days. The man recognizes

the contraband, freedom in words. They may never get another chance at
rebellion, so they color-

lines onto each other's bodies, words that will sink to
their bones. Maybe this means something,

this simple act becomes political, reading and eating words to remind them
they are flesh. They prepare

for the day their bodies will fail. Somewhere a man
and a woman write poetry to each other,

he writes *remembering* on her outer thigh. She writes
history on his chest. They write until no empty space is left.

love in a time of blood quantum

Think one-drop rule. Prove race in blood.
Each tribe, different rules. On each reservation the degree/
fraction is set you must be

¼ of the tribal blood in order to be
member, be recognized. From the beginning we grow
up knowing we are fragmented,

a life carved into quarters
and eighths of sorrow, faith, and grief. We are broken
into phases, the moon waning, never

waxing, in our fullness. Love's symptoms
became those of colonial disease (blood quantum),
always piecing ourselves together

to find an identity resembling wholeness.
If we keep mixing ourselves with each new baby, each new
love - making   lessening   blood

quantum, eliminating us
one half at   a   time.   Our brokenness
navigates like a compass

danger destined. Drawn to each other,
the deep-rooted sadness of so many things, passed down
through the body, ancestral memory, trying

to exist in two worlds. Blood
presses at the floorboards, every step we take, it's ingrained
in the earth *this land is your land*

this land is. My body's mosaic landscape contains
memories passed down in our bones. When we kiss,
we travel time – history exists in our fingertips,

colonization lingers on our lips. In love,
we are countries colliding borders, and who wants
to spend a lifetime at war.

when angels speak of love i'm pretty sure they didn't mean

drunken hockey fans spraying fifty-seven native children with beer, taunting
with racial slurs like "Go back to the reservation"

If love is all coming and going this is coloniality starting back
at its beginning with children so young they are still learning

the meaning of words like, love and hate. And you gotta hate
the way the world works when some words scar ears so deeply

that the voice that said them still echoes in your head, still
echoes in your head still echoes in your head.

Love is action and we cannot tell where an echo ends and
begins Let's think of it like this. Life begins with a woman

giving birth; because of this she is sacred. Yet,
our women are being taken. 1,181 reported missing and

murdered in Canada alone and the numbers in the US are still
unknown. Underreported not reported but we do have some

statistics: Nearly half of all Native American women have been raped,
stalked, or beaten. When angels speak of love I'm certain

they didn't mean this. Our women and children are being
traumatized. 1 in 3 Native women will be raped in her lifetime

& are 2.5 times more likely to experience sexual assault crimes
compared to all other races. When does this race to feel safe

and survive end? When you're missing in life and missing in
death, where do we begin? Nowadays

when angels try to speak of love my ears strain to hear
anything over the national news and media that barely,

if ever mention us and I wonder
if the silence is how we eventually disappear

patrick would never say the word *love*

when he volunteers to read the poem for class that day,
he does so only on the condition that he doesn't have to
say "that word." So he reads, and when he gets to
"that word" he pauses, looks at me, and waits for me
to say it [love] before continuing.

It sounds like: "the saddest thing in the world has got to be
when you [LOVE] someone unable to provide the [LOVE]
and support you need..." And I do it: dramatically, shouting.
Perhaps to make my students laugh as I fill in the gaps.

You see, Patrick, he's one of the most talented students
I've ever had. He scores his pain beautifully on the page like
he's constructing arias for operas. With poetry,
Patrick makes sense of things, his
remembering: like his mother's drinking, her suicide
attempts driving off a cliff with him at her side.
After all, what kind of mother would leave her child behind?

In another piece, Patrick calls himself a bird without wings. After class,
apologizes for always writing sad things, but
he can't help it, he says. The teacher in me tries to create
reinforcing messages like sometimes it's the sad things we need

to write in order to release, let go, break down, and cry.
I tell him "maybe try to incorporate music, I know it lifts me."
His response "But, I don't think I can sing."
I say, "Baby, it doesn't matter
whether you're on or off key it's about honoring
and using your voice." His song of choice: *I Believe I Can Fly.*

The next day he riffs between verses: *I used to think*
that I could not go on and life was nothing but
an awful song. And he hits every note.
At the back of his throat, I can hear that past anger turn
to harmonious hope and though he still won't speak it,
Patrick sings it. Later, he'll tell me
there is a difference *but now I know*
the meaning of true love.
Performing his piece inspires the quiet.
This other girl, who sits in the back of class, raises her hand,
says she also believes she's a flightless bird. But maybe
she, too, can learn to rise with music.

She asks if she can share, no longer scared, she begins
Someday I'll wish upon a star and wake up where
the clouds are far behind me. Her voice leaps off the page,
her cantatas are rage written in jagged lines to release
memories growing up in a household where
her mother's boyfriends came into her
room at night. It was then in the darkness that she
wanted to rise into flight *where troubles melt like lemon drops*
away above the chimney tops that's where you'll find me
but they pulled off her wings

as a flower de-petaled. She goes on to tell us
this continued from 3rd grade until just last year.
We are in tears when she's finished. She rips her paper,
places pieces on her tongue like sacrament, thinking
if she swallows the words this simple act might save her.
So I sit beside her, put a piece in my mouth, too.
I want her, them, the class to know
you don't have to eat your rage, pain, and sadness alone.

But they don't know I need to eat these words, too,
to feel full. Once I lost a friend who I loved
when he killed himself, his body hung from rope
like a pendulum marking the times. I never said it enough,
so today, I make sure I speak, teach, pray, and say [love]—

maybe even too much. I'll play [love] on repeat:
[my love] [my love] [my love] [my
love] when my students write pieces weighted in grief.

So when the flightless sing *birds fly over the rainbow* why *then oh*
why can't we share in experience. The class joins in, puts pieces
in their mouths, too. Together we can dissolve the heaviest ink,
turn hurt words into notes to form chords and create
a common chorus: *I believe I can fly, If I just spread my wings*

together we can fill in the gaps for those who need help
not just saying but believing in words like [love].

everything you need to know about relationships can be found in a restroom stall

Since you left me I've become obsessed
with graffiti, not the pretty wall, paint a picture
but the restroom stall scribbling, the seemingly
hurried rush in the curvature of cursive

Sometimes we forget the people we've loved or that we ever loved
anyone at all letters to get it all out. My favorites are lists:
Must See Movies or *Must Read Books*, those exquisite-corpse-
prompts to invite you in. Not so accidentally,
someone enters your life as easily and mundanely
as taking a piss. The call of nature connected in strokes
that move like a flock of birds flying away,
quit your wandering not yet knowing their destination.

It's so easy
to leave a mark behind, *remember you are beautiful —*
glimpses can be found in the dirtiest places.
And just like that out of all the restrooms in all the bars
in all the world I met, you, an anonymous passerby
who would leave nothing more than an invisible alphabet
on my forehead. Words about how not to fuck up: *don't*
make the same mistakes, or inevitable insight *I did.*

Sometimes it's too late, you've already done your business,
walked deliberately out past the scrawled inscriptions
that are more like warnings:
when did you become this person? Two extremes,
fuck you or *I am always with you,*
the pencil or permanent marker blueprint
you left behind, the dogged-eared pages of a book
with notes: *if anyone asks*

I was here etched in the margin is desire
wavering somewhere between history and the need
to fill all those empty, unoccupied spaces with
words even the nameless can say.

love on paper

Wandering the City of Chicago, I stumble
      upon the Newberry Library's exhibit titled,
            Love on Paper. It begins
                  Googled most frequently in 2014:
                  "What is love?"

Exhibit A: Archangel Gabriel. We met singing
      silly love songs from Moulin Rouge, the Eagles,
            Elton John. Was it wrong to ask
                  a stranger to duet when we were
                      drunk off red wine?

Exhibit B: The first time we made love he strummed
      melodies *Best of My Love* on guitar. We sat in the dark
            on white linen sheets so paper-thin,
                starched dry, you'd think
                    they were his wings.

Exhibit C: I don't remember the details exactly
      if Gabriel wrapped his wings around me or if I asked:
            hold me each night. *Come What May*
                rolling from his lips like waves,
                    questioning: "is this love?"

an answer my lips couldn't give as I kissed him farewell
      between wings and sheets. *Your Song* follows me in
            every city echoing beneath my ribbed cage:
                a reminder of every place my
                  paper heart has ever burned.

psalm of surrender

We reclaimed our bodies as holy,
honored each other beneath sheets, all surface
at first in our underwear too afraid to embrace
as if it was forbidden, the act. Like angels making love
with humans, like watching a lunar eclipse,
you can't, culture forbids it. Still,
you watched it on the solstice
or maybe it watched you, the moon
mimicking the private parts. Inside us the sun flickers
bright shades of sorrow into our veins.
Not unlike rivers, they surrender
to the ocean. We detect the sadness
in the waves blowing kisses to the coveted shoreline
as they sway towards and away
refusing to stay. Longing flows in whispered repetition
inside our blood, reminding us we are humans who believe
we can wait outside churches on Sundays
for people to hand out forgiveness
like pennies destined for wells. We wish
we could skip across the surface, the universe
of our bodies, or sing a psalm
delicate enough to be placed
in our palms that touch. The gravity inside
our voices forms an imperfect chord
that resonates throughout the bodily halls,
lost in each other's kingdom's we forget to pray
to the angels. But, each night we dream we are
butterflies grounded from flight, begging the angels
to fix our winged bodies.

somewhere being written

i'm convinced someone somewhere is painting the moon

        stretching its canvas to extend from

one planet to the next. angels & saints cover it in hues that

        encompass galaxies – the heavy

pigment even tempts lost planets into

        orbit. paper-thin i am pulled in

to the linen that begs for lines

        so i rearrange constellations,

suspend a message on

        the Milky Way. we all need

to believe in something bigger than

        ourselves – ask: *are there limits?*

to loving, the sky responds *halfway to ecstasy we forget*

        we are ever star-far away, two hands

searching for each other. in the dark, the moon grasps

        at oceans and we envy the ability

to rise, not knowing the moon mourns, unable

to keep waves from leaving

the shoreline. strangers wish upon

fallen stars never looking up

to listen. the moon hums

repetitively *come back to me,*

come back to me, come back

to me, a prayer so near silence we can barely

hear the lift into daylight as it carries us

away from this life into the next.

excavation

I read once that an echo could be excavated. It wasn't so easy
to unearth history: take an art historian and audio engineer

to figure out how
to reconfigure

and create experiences. It happened once
in a basilica named Hagia Sophia.

It took not one, but two people to recreate the voices.
Calculating the calibrations, they popped balloons

to determine the distance and time it takes such breaking
to travel. From one side to the next, past to present. How long

the vowels rounded out expanding to smokey *O*'s
o   o o   o o O   O O O o filling every inch of the room

with echoes. It takes two people
to dig into the past. If

our bodies are temples can we recreate
the sounds of our break —

ing? Ours happened
like balloons, all the things we left

unsaid filling our throats until they exploded
sounds of broken bottles, glass shattering onto

concrete sidewalks you ran away on into a night that ended
with your neck breaking, your body

a question hanging from rope the last sound
though maybe it was more of a cry, a weeping

out of our mouths, yours a pained & mine wailing,
O.

IV. THE ORDER OF THINGS

Courage did not come from the need to survive, or from a brute indifference inherited from someone else, but from a driving need for love which no obstacle in this world or the next world will break.

– Gabriel García Márquez, *Love in a Time of Cholera*

i write this
withoutbreakingmyheart

the order of things

The bird's nest fallen from tree: a single egg remaining,
you, me. We cracked in curiosity wanting to see
what it looked like — birth or death, maybe both
before we really knew either. We wondered. Was it still
alive, heart beating, bird, body, breathing?

We fought over who would be first to break before deciding
it came down to courage. Whoever had the most would be
the one: *you*, tapped the shell, each movement attuned
to our attempts at silent, measured breath, and then inside:
an unexpected baby bird, mouth slightly open

in muted calls, so small, delicate, helpless. You held it, then I.
We passed its damp body back and forth until it eventually
dried a blur on the sidewalk. Childhood events fragment
as years pass, the brain self protects against the order of things.
We can only imagine different trajectories,

a newspaper that reads: *one of the leading causes of death for all
ages is heart disease,* an article leading into the obituaries:
yours. Silently, I process unexpected years, what's left
behind, how we felt before experiencing the dryness
of death. How courageous we were back then,

cor, meaning heart, ours unbearably bound
by the weight of our ever-fragile shells.

please remember me

he writes the word *temperance*
on my body. the way one studies

for a test memorizing my body's curves.
we drink each other in, his bitterness

cloaks my despair. he subtracts six letters
and adds six more to spell *temptation.*

the angles of the body — i am not equal
to the sum of my original parts. *scarred.*

did you know if you take out one of the r's...
i get *scared* when he asks

have you ever had wings? he traces his fingertips
over them questioning the scars'

identical lengths, the equal spacing
on my upper back. he writes _____

a formula for intimacy, something only he can see
in the dark. we try to go back to our beginnings,

fill in the disconnections and blanks.
but, he can't deal in imaginary

letters or numbers. maybe i am imaginary
and he is real. we slowly love ourselves

out of existence, combine our clay bodies.
twist and mold into one imperfect lump,

struggling to shape shift into each other
's complex pasts. we can change the words,

the history we carry. describing time travel
his fingers trail the length of my body pausing along

my thigh like stops on a train. city to city
all the way up to my neck he caresses

a kiss to mark each stop along
a journey destined for elsewhere.

teaching the riff

mamas put in Davis during children's naps
time to let the miles of music unfold into sleeping ears.
mamas fear this world where babies are born

already confined, waiting in lines of funeral processions,
the patient air reinforces lessons of Indians playing along
to historically provided scores, the notes read: broken

livers, diseased hearts, and distended bellies
in newspapers or television. babies need the music,
the rhythm and blues teach improvisation, the realization:

life is making and creating. embedded in the call and
response of crying shames reside voracious
cold trains, bodies freighted with ache.

mamas wanna teach children the riff between
what goes on outside these man-made borders,
the 'real' world where cars are named after Indians:

Navajo, Cherokee, and Tacoma; they know
the consequences of the American Dream. reality:
just like those cars they too will end up buried

in graveyards; if they're not careful sooner than expected
so mamas pray their children dream blues like cracked cups.
broken may not be good luck but reminds us

of survival, an object lesson: if you leave, leave blaring
like trumpet, dented in all the places to sound your instrument
loud for the trail of knowing behind you. history's riffs

may be blinding but babies need reminding
when arms are strong enough to unravel muddy
waters still needing to be crossed they are ready to embrace

the splitting open like saxophone howling into the white
space or ocean all to empty the darkness inside
or to fill it with their own middle ground between

the milestones and giant steps they'll want to make in life.
so whenever they think blues can be tasted with hands
wrapped around bottle until they're wasted

they'll remember their mama's ingrained into their hearts
unexpected deviations, their internal drums will beat
louder than the drunken syncopations as they fall

into no longer sweet grass laying flat on backs
looking up at the Indian in the moon,
in their sweat drenched sourness loving

and wondering what's so damn
wonderful about a world where we
are whole notes unraveling.

if there is something to

longing, broken could mean something
simple and innocent like puzzles put together
only to be taken apart again. What are the chances

the universe would bring A and B together, with
B already broken beyond saving. From his own
deliberate fragmentation, without A,
B does not know what to follow.

Consider the geometry: piece together a shape
where *Person A* misses *Person B*
by 90-degrees. When A slightly angles away
from B, what happens?

Measure the length when
A and B embrace, see if their bodies
rearrange into a spatial metaphor
about loss and love, as one
tries to call the other
before someone
must let go.

some kind of dying

morning coffee can be laced with too much

happiness for moments like this, where I can't help but

focus on the length of your wingspan. Your arms must be long

to have reached me who keeps everyone at more than

a birds' eye view. *When I say eternity I don't mean forever.*

I mean specificity like a necklace, the distance I wear.

You and I, too static, two-dimensional representations of

three words I dare not say, may cause a break

in dimensional space: your hands pour coffee, down my throat,

hoping it will expand wide enough to break the necklace,

tightly holding on.

post-flight assessment: the call of urgency

it starts with an untangling—
he hung himself, the Emergency
      medical technicians and police declared

on scene. his body, post-flight
assess the condition, they'd said,
      broken neck. closed airway. no breathing. no

circulation. body immobilized. bone
fractured. the *rigor* already set in.
      too late for technical rescue. like a solitary

crow hops back and forth, back
and forth he must have paced
      the length of the stairwell like a runway

before casting out his song
wrapped in flight's urgency.
      mouth to sky. ear to wind he must have

listened before deciding gravity
never existed before he extended
      his wings to a length of loneliness and jumped—

Some circumstances call
for such gestures. Around
      us, all the distant birds sensed the change,

the wind's unintended weight
as they cleared the scene and we
      all struggled to rise towards the barely visible sun.

awakening: you died while i was sleeping

and I climbed further and farther into the night to ask the
stars: are there limits to loving? In silence they answered.

Unspoken, I placed grief on the backs of constellations
rearranged my thinking, put together the lights to make

the sky read: *people grow up, out of love, and leave people behind.*
You left. I lost you when you died and maybe

yes, maybe love can be rendered in the countless times
I awoke that night to hear your voice crying

on the wind that carried it or was it my own
that woke me as it echoed *Come back to me.*

Come back to me. Come back to me. You died
while I was sleeping and I can't remember

what I was dreaming about,
if I was dreaming at all.

never meant to touch

None of this was supposed to happen. I imagine
the Creator only meant for us to be moments —
dying and rebirth waiting to be shaped
with tongue. It could have been a test to understand the gift

of voice. What it means to be messengers — like the Angels
who constantly try to open our eyes by waiting.
Outside stores, homeless men sit hands extended toward us,
palm up as if holding all life's secrets just in the act

of asking. Or a baby born in a tiny body with hands
already grasping at the world. Perhaps the Angels tried to warn us of what's
not meant to be, like butterflies whose
wings lose their shimmer through a human touch,
not knowing something so simple could kill us.

unchained melody

Saint Francis saw me crying outside of a bookstore
near the entrance. I wouldn't have noticed
if it hadn't been for him tapping my shoulder
proclaiming, "This place isn't big enough"
before he sideways stepped through

the opened glass door spilling out
Nina Simone's *blackbird* voice
why you wanna fly. Signs.
I'd always believed in them.

Grounded for years after Angel took his leap
and fell unintentionally clipping my wings.
I might've leapt then if Francis hadn't returned
with paper and a pen to sit beside me.

So I asked, "Francis, what do we do with the lonely?"
And he sang, "The same thing you do with pain"
Our eyes are endless wells big enough
for holding every fallen star's light.

And I started to write all the tears I had
already cried, wondering: is it possible
for any of us to ever love, again?

measure by measure: the body begs

at the soul's release *please do not leave.*
The last crescendo breathing and
the body intertwined, two hands
offered as a gesture like grasping at butterflies,
longing to hold something precious.
The legatos of trying
hear the search in continuous acts,
the staccatoed beats.
Dal capo al coda,
go back to the beginning
in the music of being human,
the final score and the counterpoint:
hands outstretched as if to say
I cannot stay

consider the assemblage of a longing

rendered in stone so distinct it should be studied not quite
       unlike Orpheus
and Eurydice who tried to return to the land of the living –
       El Parque del Amor
and *El Beso* should be a part of this body of myths
       like Rodin's *Kiss*,
the book in Paolo's hand, a near-miss of lips, the mouth
       opens a cyclone, breaths
barely separated as the space between pages. But,
       we are not gods,
monsters, or heroes – just two unnamed bodies in history.
       And maybe
in the land of the living it is certain one lover will always try
       to look back,
to call the other the way the moon begs constellations
       to rearrange
their stars into monuments assembled in longing.

the significance of a hanging

It seems so simple, cleaning, a meaningless act.
                                            Hanging

on my east facing wall the star quilt gifted to me
                                            it came from

your funeral where it hung across the length of
                                            an ocean —

a long rope lovingly stretched from me on one
                                            side, you

the other, resting in unrecognizable sleep. Your
                                            face,

expressions, never looked that way. The first
                                            years of

let's not call it *grieving*, but seeing the significance of
                                            forgiveness

the quilt reminded me of home, of you, of each
                                            direction

east, west, north, and south. I hung it as a daily
                                            reminder

tack by tack, I put it up, let it hang for a year
                                            as a prayer

of remembrance. Until I received the next one at
                                            your

memorial, another quilt this one splashed in

                                    colors

your brightness: oranges, yellows, and blues

                                   the hues

trying to exist together. I remember

                                   nights

I covered myself with the quilts as if they were

                                   you

covering me with courage and grace or humility.

                                   By wounds

words, by root and sky, you linked us. I finally

                                   found

you that day I came home to knowing connection

                                   in breathing

The same way you did that day, I hung it then

                                   in steps

I needed to take it down, tack by tack and

                                   when

the final ones could no longer bear the weight

                                   I let you fall.

the milky way escapes my mouth

whenever two lips begin to form your name
I cough stars lodged deep within my lungs. They rush
                    from tongue weighted in dust, words
                                        I didn't ask

where are you going? or notice the blank spaces
in your breathing as you slept. They say
                    the more massive the star, the shorter
                                        the lifespan.

They have greater pressure on their cores. Yours burned
so brightly I should have known you'd collapse, disappear
                    into image, a black hole dissolving
                                        trace amounts.

I am left stargazing five times a day for years. Catalogue
phrases. Chart each word. Label every facial expression.
                    Telescope until eyes bleed constellations
                                        even then

I can't navigate my way into understanding light years –
how we let darkness slip in. Is it madness to wonder
                    if it ever really happened? You, a shadow never
                                        leaving until I

inserted continents between us. *I lost you* in the crevice
between night and day. You died while I was sleeping
                    dreaming of a galaxy far far away where
                                        love eclipses.

A rising tide of longing fills my body, bones, the ribs
sheltering the cave within me echoing. Each night,
                    I open mouth sky-wide to swallow stars
                                        and sing

to the moon a story about the light of two people
who continue to cross and uncross in their falling
                no matter how unstable
                                in orbit.

we were once two stars

the first cordiform map was produced in 1519 by Oronce Fine

Angel spoke the language of stars,
filled my eyes with breathable light.

He said it was the sadness in human voices
that drew him to us, the way the hurt

somehow forms an imperfect chord
that resonated throughout the hall of

our bodily kingdoms. Angel and I exist
together on other planes, in past lives, and

futures to follow. Angel is a love wish.
In each life we choose each other.

I spent years waiting in this life for him to
find me and see. We both believed in the healing

of broken hearts through song.
In each existence, we write

music & lyrics on each other's backs,
a cordiform map hidden in invisible ink

so our bodies remember how to always find our way
back to each other. On the otherside,

ours is a Love Story already written
for those who in the end, need to live and

love in a time of blood quantum
feeling utterly and completely whole.

winter – birds of flight

Even when grandmother gifted me my name I didn't believe
I was capable of flight. Winter Bird sang deep in my veins
she heard it the moment I came from womb and pierced the air
with cries in praise of breath. But I felt the weight of

winter, of water. I didn't know when she sang, prayers
washed over me. When the wings started to grow from
my back I tried to fly. The first time, I climbed
on our shed and jumped only to fall. Mother said
I was still an eaglet, not ready to soar just yet.
The broken wing from that crash

landing began my journey falling again and again.
As I grew older I wanted to fly, follow my own direction,
but wondered if I came from sand and stone. After you died
I sloughed off my wings in layers, peeling an apple
until I reached the core. Abandoned flight.

I used to believe the stone part of me pulled you
down, that's why you fell swinging from rope, your body
the pendulum that finally ended your time on earth?

I wanted to fly to you then but could only put words
to paper an airplane I folded to send
back in history, to save you, save us.
In an opera version your death would be beautiful
on stage with sonatas of

sacrifice. The final act
would generate enough tears,
the flightless would sprout wings.
Maybe then we would believe:
we are born from folding
and reborn in the unfolding.

back to the beginning

sometimes i wish we could start back
at the beginning. turn our existence into a videotape
call it *Life*. then push *Life* into a VCR.
press PLAY then PAUSE and get the chance to
REWIND with our image still on screen
watching everything that ever meant anything reverse
with the push of a finger.

if we could press REWIND
the wrinkles on these God given shells would smooth
into soft unscathed skin. we'd awaken from tombs,
arise from the earth like trees living to become seeds,
and i guess that means as babies we'd go back in to our mother's wombs.

if we could press REWIND
mothers or fathers who abandoned
their daughters or sons wouldn't walk away but return,
run backwards turning towards their children.
then they'd never have to look into eyes
that ever saw them as unworthy of keeping.
history wouldn't repeat, but instead fold into itself
like disease-ridden blankets rolling themselves back up
like yo-yos returning to the hands that made those hateful gestures
in the first place. battles wouldn't end
in bloodshed, but instead a ride off into a sun rising
with warriors always returning from war
or boarding schools with their hair flowing behind them in lengths of rivers.

REWINDing, would mean
handing in our diplomas & going back to school
to unlearn all the lessons ever taught to us. we'd start
books at their ending, unstring sentences into letters until
all we were left with was sound waiting
to come out of our mouths. like my friend Angel,
his would open to fountain gallons of vodka
from liver, his throat would spill it back into bottle
after bottle after bottle after bottle
that he'd set back onto the shelves of a liquor store
he'd walk out of in a line so straight it'd lead him
to the day Angel's father cut off his wings when he left him,
fatherless, falling asleep on a bench.

REWINDing,
he'd unfreeze to death as warmth re-entered
his body convulsing not in dry heaving but reheating
detoxing into calm as snowflakes would slowly rise back up to the sky.
the kind of miracle time travel – imagine,
needles sucking poisonous drugs from addicted veins, pills
un-dissolving into wholeness being pushed back into containers
fitting just right. everything would be all right.
especially for our youth who contemplated taking their own lives
or committed suicide would feel blood flow back into open cuts,
their veins pulsing with life that knows it's worth saving
so much that determined hands repeatedly pull away razors
from wrists until every scar slowly disappeared leaving behind no trace,
not even the memory. and every fist that hit someone in rage or abuse
would loosen into outstretched arms to call you home
instead of the bullet shaped holes being shot into bodies
making their way back into the guns or mouths
that shot them in the first place.

if we could REWIND
maybe i could remember
if i ever said anything to hurt Angel.

if we could REWIND,
my Angel would be able to fly
backwards, defy gravity, lift himself up and
life would be breathed back into him
as he unwrapped the rope from his neck
to inhale sweet and ever expanding air into his chest.

if we could REWIND
i could tell Angel, over & over *i loved you*
and it would always always start with —
you, alive & well and not me.
i'd give up every poem i have ever spoken,
have my mouth call back each and every one of them
from your ears back into my pen
's failed attempts at putting back together
all the splintered pieces of our
hearts our hearts our hearts
our hearts staring at a blank page,
wishing we could

begin again.

Acknowledgments

I am indebted to the editors of the following journals for publishing (in some version) poems from this collection:

Adobe Walls: "Broken Tulips" and "Preface to Lost Intimacies," "Rhapsody in Reservation Blues," and "The Significance of a Hanging," (nominated for a Pushcart Prize)

Cutthroat Magazine: "A Story About Winter," "When Angels Speak of Love," and "The Milky Way Escapes My Mouth"

Drunken Boat #15: "In the Age of Doubt," "Broken Hymn: To the Offset Metronome," and "Language Less Learning"

Duke City Fix: "In My Mother's Womb", "Ten Little Indians"

Lingerpost: "Softly: How to Evaporate"

Malpais Review: "The Weight of Water," "When We Banish Tongues," "Sometimes I Dream a Reservation Resides Inside Me," "Post-Flight Assessment: The Call of Urgency," and "Love in a Time of Blood Quantum."

Superstition Review: "Consider the Assemblage of a Longing" and "the body begs"

Yellow Medicine Review: "Reflections of the Moon," "The Textures of Silence," "The War on Words," and "Surrender to Memory"

San Diego Poetry Annual: "Learning to Say I Love You" and "Sonnet MCLXXXI"

Kweli: "What John Wayne Couldn't Have Known"

Toe Good Poetry: "Patrick Would Never Say The Word Love"

Ishaan Literary Review: "The Order of Things," and "Everything You Need to Know About Relationships"

As/Us: A Space for Women of the World: "Somewhere Being Written"

And Love (anthology by Jacar Press): "Some Kind of Dying"

In addition, I am honored that "The Impermanence of Human Sculptures" won the Spring 2012 Orlando Prize in Poetry from A Room Of Her Own Foundation. The Poetic Theater Productions Company in New York performed "When Angels Speak of Love" in the show *Love, Redefined Poetic License 2015*. Poetic Theater Productions also performed *"Somewhere Being Written," "W(hole): Self-Medication," "Ten Little Indians"* and ten poems featured in this collection and in a previous rendition as "Love in a Time of Blood Quantum." "The Order of Things" was part of *Emotive Fruition* at the Bowery Poetry Club in New York.

First and foremost, I thank the Creator for giving me life and for gifting me this purpose. Thank you for making me a vessel for words like love.

I want to thank my family for showing me unconditional love. I want to thank my Grandpa Allen for unfolding the world to me, encouraging me to look to the stars in all their magic. You helped me dream much bigger than I could have dreamed alone. Thank you for believing in me and for helping me believe that I could do anything. Losing you was one of the hardest things I've had to endure, but you guided me to a lifetime of learning and poetry. Thank you Uncle Neman - you made me believe my voice was worth sharing every time you wanted to listen to me sing songs. Thank you, grandma for your kindness, resiliency, strength, stories, and songs. You let me read you to sleep when I was just a little girl searching for words and you gave me song. Thank you MOM for your guidance, strength, and advice. You are my light in the darkest of nights; my rock when I need support. I want to thank my sister Natahnee. You are my best friend. You continually teach me about the kind of person I want to be – loving and giving without condition. You make me want to be a better person. Thank you Dad for teaching me that love is a force capable of stopping time.

Thank you Professor Gabrielle Calvocoressi (my first poetry teacher at Stanford) for introducing me to *The Art of Losing,* which cracked open my heart like an ice pick to the chest creating an endless hole through which poetry flows. Because of you I know I will spend a lifetime writing the same poem over and over just in different ways.

Thank you Professor Eavan Boland for teaching my young-still-searching-for-herself-and-words self. I am grateful that I somehow ended up in your course that quarter to hear you talk about Blake's *Tyger Tyger burning bright*. You taught me about the pauses after the white space and made me appreciate that breaking a line could break my breath to make words resonate.

Thanks to Li Young Lee for teaching me that poetry is alchemy. Your teachings about poetry being of the dying breath forever changed my craft. Thanks to Robert Pinsky for teaching me about the etymology and the importance of the sounds in every word we use in a poem.

Thank you to my maestra Cherrie Moraga – you taught me that *Loving in the War Years* was no easy task but that love is an act of courage. Thank you for encouraging me to take action. Your class and tutelage helped me find *duende* and unearth the voice I'd always been afraid to share.

For my mentor Joy Harjo who showed me to be *Crazy Brave*; you have helped me be unafraid of everything that comes my way. You help me realize everything happens for a reason. Thank you for your guidance, light, and friendship. You have helped lay a foundation by passing on so much more than I could ever thank you for.

Thanks to Peter Campion, Alexandra Teague, Dana Levin, Dan Mueller, Greg Martin, Ruth Ellen Kocher, and Michelle Otero. Thank you Marlon and Casandra for being my literary soulmates. Your poetry and words have saved me again and again. Thank you David and Diahndra – your friendship and encouragement has meant the world to me. Thank you Chris for being my "life coach." To Scott, thank you for helping me understand what it means to be seen and find healing. Much light and appreciation to Angela Sterritt, thank you for sharing your beautiful gifts and talents in this world and for allowing me to use one on the cover of this book. Thank you Profesora y Directora Irene Vasquez for allowing me to teach again – you helped me remember my purpose by allowing me to serve the students we write for.

Thank you Maurice. "Mo" you are every moment I wish I could live again and every memory I want to slow down. You are the breath I am grateful to take. Thank you for teaching me that memory is one of the most powerful, fragile things. You taught me falling and gave me the strength to pull myself out of the art of forgetfulness. Because of you I can now bravely and without fear say, "I remember..."

Thanks to Indigenous Services at Western University and Susan and Rick for supporting my family and me. Thanks to my Dream Warriors family (Frank Waln, Mic Jordan, and Tall Paul) for helping me understand the responsibility we have in using the gifts we've been given. Thank you for reminding me to always act out of and from a place of love. Each of you inspires me to want to create. Frank, thank you for being my safe harbor – your music and friendship has helped me find the strength to finally finish this book.

Thank you to CU Upward Bound (CUUB), all my students (aka CUUBs) and Native Youth I've been able to meet, read to, perform for, and teach along the way. I write my heart onto pages for each of you in hopes of guiding you to follow the light you already hold in your hands. You are powerful beyond measure. You are destined for something great. With all of your gifts, you will make the world beautiful again.

Thank you to all my former teachers, students, friends, and supporters. Thank you for believing in me.

To Angel: Thank you for showing me love is not a destination on a map, but rather an unglobable practice. I hope you find everything you're searching for. I hope you get what you need.

And finally, to every person I love(d) – thank you for the lessons my time with you taught me. Without you, I wouldn't have been able to write these words.